FOREX TRA
The Beginners G
Big With Forex T

Compiled and Written By
By Larry E."Buck" Hunter

FOREX TRAINING
The Beginners Guide to Making It Big With Forex Trading Compiled by Larry E. "Buck" Hunter
© 2015 by **Larry E. "Buck" Hunter**
All Rights Reserved.   No part of this publication may be reproduced in any form or by any means, including scanning, photocopying, or otherwise without prior written permission of the copyright holder.

First Printing, 2015

Printed in the United States of America

Terms of Use
You are given a non-transferable, "personal use" license to this product. You can share it with other individuals

PUBLISHED BY
ECONO PUBLISHING, LLC
6599 Kuna Road, Kuna, Idaho 83634
(208) 402-8822
E-mail:admin@econopublishing.com
Website: www.econopublishing.com

TABLE OF CONTENTS

RISKS ASSOCIATED WITH FOREX TRAINING 5
RISK DISCLAIMER 6
DISCLAIMER OF ENDORSEMENT 7
LEGAL NOTICE 8
INTRODUCTION TO THE FOREX 9
    WHAT IS FOREX? 9
    WHO TRADES CURRENCIES? 9
    WHY TRADE FOREX? 10
Chapter 1: 11
What the Stock Market is All About 11
Chapter 2: 19
Stock Market Trends 19
Chapter 3: 24
An Introduction to Forex 24
Chapter 4: 30
Understanding Currency Conversion 30
Chapter 5: 35
Understanding Statistics 35
Chapter 6: 40
Forex Volatility and Market Expectation 40
Chapter 7: 45
Aspects of The Trade 45
Chapter 8: 49
Risk Management 49
Chapter 9: 54
Buzz Words 54
Chapter 10: 60
Expert Trading Options 60
Chapter 11: 64
Other Trading Options 64
Chapter 12: 69
In Review 69
Chapter 13: 74
One Final Option 74
FREE COURSE: LEARN TO TRADE CURRENCY 76

RISKS ASSOCIATED WITH FOREX TRADING (Please Read)

Trading foreign currencies can be a challenging and potentially profitable opportunity for investors. However, before deciding to participate in the Forex market, you should carefully consider your investment objectives, level of experience, and risk appetite. Most importantly, do not invest money you cannot afford to lose.

There is considerable exposure to risk in any foreign exchange transaction. **ANY TRANSACTION INVOLVING CURRENCIES INVOLVES RISKS INCLUDING, BUT NOT LIMITED TO, AND THE POTENTIAL FOR CHANGING POLITICAL AND/OR ECONOMIC CONDITIONS THAT MAY SUBSTANTIALLY AFFECT THE PRICE OR LIQUIDITY OF A CURRENCY.** Investments in foreign exchange speculation may also be susceptible to sharp rises and falls as the relevant market values fluctuate.

The leveraged nature of Forex trading means that any market movement will have an equally proportional effect on your deposited funds. This may work against you as well as for you. Not only may investors get back less than they invested, but in the case of higher risk strategies, investors may lose the entirety of their investment. It is for this reason that when speculating in such markets it is advisable to use only risk capital.

RISK DISCLAIMER (Please Read)

TRADING FOREIGN EXCHANGE ON MARGIN CARRIES A HIGH LEVEL OF RISK, AND MAY NOT BE SUITABLE FOR ALL INVESTORS.

Past performance is not indicative of future results. The high degree of leverage can work against you as well as for you. Before deciding to invest in foreign exchange you should carefully consider your investment objectives, level of experience, and risk appetite.

The possibility exists that you could sustain a loss of some or all of your initial investment and therefore you should not invest money that you cannot afford to lose. You should be aware of all the risks associated with foreign exchange trading, and seek advice from an independent financial advisor if you have any doubts.

DISCLAIMER OF ENDORSEMENT
(Please Read)

REFERENCE HEREIN TO ANY SPECIFIC WEBSITE, COMMERCIAL PRODUCTS, PROCESS, OR SERVICE BY TRADE NAME, TRADEMARK, MANUFACTURER, OR OTHERWISE, DOES NOT NECESSARILY CONSTITUTE OR IMPLY ITS ENDORSEMENT, RECOMMENDATION, OR FAVORING TO THE **PUBLISHER OR THE AUTHOR/COMPILER** OF THE E-BOOK.

The views and opinions of the Publisher or the author/compiler expressed herein does not necessarily state or reflect those of any specific website, commercial products, process, or service by trade name, trademark or manufacturer and shall not be used for advertising or product endorsement purposes.

With respect to websites and other resource materials inserted and available in this e-book the Publisher and the author/compiler makes no warranty, express or implied to its accuracy, including the warranties of merchantability and fitness for a particular purpose; **NOR DOES THE PUBLISHER OR THE AUTHOR/COMPILER ASSUME ANY LEGAL LIABILITY OR RESPONSIBILITY FOR THE ACCURACY, COMPLETENESS, OR USEFULNESS OF ANY INFORMATION, APPARATUS, PRODUCT, OR PROCESS DISCLOSED IN THIS E-BOOK.**

LEGAL NOTICE (Please Read)

The Publisher and the author/compiler has strived to be as accurate and complete as possible in the creation of this report, notwithstanding the fact that he does not warrant or represent at any time that the contents within are accurate due to the rapidly changing nature of the Internet.

WHILE ALL ATTEMPTS HAVE BEEN MADE TO VERIFY INFORMATION PROVIDED IN THIS PUBLICATION, THE PUBLISHER AND THE AUTHOR/COMPILER ASSUMES NO RESPONSIBILITY FOR ERRORS, OMISSIONS, OR CONTRARY INTERPRETATION OF THE SUBJECT MATTER HEREIN. ANY PERCEIVED SLIGHTS OF SPECIFIC PERSONS, PEOPLES, OR ORGANIZATIONS ARE UNINTENTIONAL.

In practical advice books, like anything else in life, **THERE ARE NO GUARANTEES OF INCOME MADE.** Readers are cautioned to reply on their own judgment about their individual circumstances to act accordingly.

THIS BOOK IS NOT INTENDED FOR USE AS A SOURCE OF LEGAL, BUSINESS, ACCOUNTING OR FINANCIAL ADVICE.
All readers are advised to seek services of competent professionals in legal, business, accounting and finance fields.

INTRODUCTION TO THE FOREX

http://www.forex.com/why-trade-forex.html

WHAT IS FOREX?

"**For**eign **ex**change; it's also known as FX. In a forex trade, you buy one currency while simultaneously selling another - that is, you're exchanging the sold currency for the one you're buying. The foreign exchange market is an over-the-counter market.

Currencies trade in pairs, like the Euro-US Dollar (EUR/USD) or US Dollar / Japanese Yen (USD/JPY). Unlike stocks or futures, there's no centralized exchange for forex. All transactions happen via phone or electronic network.

WHO TRADES CURRENCIES?

Daily turnover in the world's currencies comes from two sources:

- **Foreign trade (5%).** Companies buy and sell products in foreign countries, plus convert profits from foreign sales into domestic currency.

- **Speculation** for profit **(95%).** Most traders focus on the biggest, most liquid currency pairs. "**The Majors**" include US Dollar, Japanese Yen, Euro, British Pound, Swiss Franc, Canadian Dollar and Australian Dollar. In fact, more than 85% of daily forex trading happens in the major currency pairs.

WHY TRADE FOREX?

With average daily turnover of US $5 trillion, forex is the most traded financial market in the world.

A true 24-hour market from Sunday 5 PM ET to Friday 5 PM ET, forex trading begins in Sydney, and moves around the globe as the business day begins, first to Tokyo, London, and New York.

Unlike other financial markets, investors can respond immediately to currency fluctuations, whenever they occur - day or night.

FOREIGN EXCHANGE

The Federal Reserve Bank of New York (http://www.ny.frb.org/) carries out foreign exchange-related activities on behalf of the Federal Reserve System and the U.S. Treasury. In this capacity, the Bank monitors and analyzes global financial market developments, manages the U.S. foreign currency reserves, and from time to time intervenes in the foreign exchange market. The Bank also executes foreign exchange transactions on behalf of customers.

http://en.wikipedia.org/wiki/Federal_Reserve_Bank_of_New_York

Chapter 1:

What the Stock Market is All About

(http://en.wikipedia.org/wiki/Stock_market)

In any business or moneymaking venture, preparation and foreknowledge are the keys to success. Without this sort of insight, the attempt to make a profitable financial decision can only end in disaster and failure, regardless of your level of motivation and determination or the amount of money you plan to invest.
In the stock market, this rule applies to the nth degree, as you are investing your own money in what could be considered a high risk wager, and you are playing with fire if you do not have at least a general background knowledge of how it functions.

Since having a background in any area is helpful in guiding you down a path in that particular region, the more solid your basis of investment knowledge is, the more likely you are to profit from any attempt to trade on the open market.
In many ways, trading on the stock market can be compared to driving – you do not have to be an expert to get behind the wheel of a car, though you are expected to have some previous knowledge about basic traffic laws, including moving violations, safety regulations, and other legal vehicular infractions, which are learned through either specific study and coursework or

even through some form of simple exposure (such as the years you have spent riding with your parents and others who have driven for years).

You should be able to comprehend the basic tools used to navigate a car (where the brake pedal is located versus the gas, and how to use the rearview mirror, for example), even if you have never touched a steering wheel.

The same is true in entering the world of the stock market or FOREX Trading.

While you do not have to know all the terminology (you will not be short selling or determining your own long and short positions at first, so you do not have to understand these references completely, though you should be aware of them), you should certainly be versed in the basic functionality of trading stocks, bonds, securities, and other commodities.

And just like someone who is behind the wheel of a car and getting ready to touch the gas pedal for the first time, you should start out with caution and work your way in slowly. A first time driver will first set the mirrors to his or her own liking, then put the car in gear, look for any interfering traffic, and ease onto the gas pedal, never flooring it and testing the engine coming out of the gate on the first attempt.

Likewise, when you select your first investment, you should choose something stable with little fluctuation and not invest a large sum of money on this first venture.

When a person is learning to drive, he or she will be accompanied by another individual who is more experienced and can assist them in making better driving decisions and offering corrections that will aid in learning to handle the car more efficiently. In the stock market, there are stockbrokers and other experts who can give you input and advice to help you in building your knowledge of the commodities in which you are interested, essentially "steering" you toward better stock market buying and selling decisions.

You could spend hours and hours researching the stock market and its functionality, learning how to become involved in the trade and who to contact to get in the game, especially if your interest lies in the Foreign Exchange Market, which goes far beyond the level of complication of the domestic stock market.

However, in this book, you will find all the basic information you need to get started down the path to trading success.

All of the leg work and tough research has been done for you, collecting the data and knowledge into one source from which you can gain enough insight to make you a successful trader on the open market.

All you have to do is read in order to gain knowledge and wisdom, step by step that will bring you to a heady level of success. In this e-book, you will find all such helpful information, all brought together in one single source for ease of reference.

HOW INVESTMENT WORKS
(INVESTING 101: WHAT IS INVESTING?
http://www.investopedia.com/university/beginner/beginner1.asp)

Any time you are going to be putting your money into a fund; it is a good idea to start by understanding what you are buying into.
The stock market is a complicated entity, and doing minimal business in trading requires a fair amount of basic knowledge, as well as the understanding and acceptance of the high risk factor.

The more you know in advance regarding the functionality of the system, the less likely it is that you will take a heavy hit, ending in devastating loss.

First of all and probably most important in the trading business, you should understand what stocks actually are. When you buy or sell a stock on the open market, you should keep in mind that you are dealing with real objects, not pieces of paper; you are buying and selling real parts of a particular company, its product, or some other various commodity.

Owning a "share" means that you have actually bought into the company or product involved and become a partial owner of that commodity. Of course, you could be one of millions of shareholders, as most companies and products are broken into minute pieces of the whole, but you are still considered an investor in that company or product until you sell your shares.

Think of it as paying for a tank of gas in the car that your parents bought for you to drive. You may have even bought the oil filter that has been put on the car, and you may feel that this investment makes you part owner.

However, when you look at the overall cost of the car, you have really contributed very little to that amount. However, as long as you continue to invest in the gas for the car and take care of the maintenance needs, you can claim part ownership of the car.

Because the value of a company and its products or services can fluctuate continuously, the value of the stocks you hold will not be the same from day to day and can sometimes even change hourly. When the price per share drops and is considered low, it is an ideal time to purchase.

This is the least expensive way to begin your trading venture, and working with a stock broker will allow you to gain more information as to what stocks are ripe for the purchase at any given time.

In doing so, you become a stockholder, and the value of your holdings will fluctuate from day to day.

Your gamble (and hope!) is that the value of the company or product in which you have invested will increase or rebound from the low price at which you made your purchase. This is the goal of all traders and means that your stock will become more valuable.

As the value of your securities increases, so does your net worth. When the price of the stock in your possession reaches a high point, it is time to sell, making a profit on your original investment. Ideally, you will always sell your holdings for a reasonably higher price than the purchase amount and should never sell when the current value of the stock is below your initial purchase price.

It is important to make sure that you do not purposely take a net loss because there are plenty of occasions when you could be forced to take a loss.

For example, if you purchase shares of a company at twenty dollars each, you should never sell them for eighteen dollars apiece. If possible, you want to hold off until they are each worth perhaps forty dollars, in essence doubling your money. Of course, this is just an example, and not all stocks will ever double in value, but the illustration is meaningful.

There are other, more complex ways to invest in the stock market. However, much like learning to ride a bicycle, you do not want to make your first attempt without training wheels.

MAKING DECISIONS - THE BEGINNING

Let us return to driving as a reference. When you first start driving, you will not enter the highway and take the car at speeds of sixty and seventy miles per hour. Instead, you will stay in residential areas or at least on the access road, where there is less pressure to maintain such a high speed. In the stock market, you will also want to stay away from any expensive stocks or extremely volatile investments until you have become extremely comfortable with the process of trading.

PENNY STOCKS

There are small investment opportunities referred to as **"PENNY STOCKS"**, (http://www.investopedia.com/ask/answers/03/072503.asp) which will help you try out your sea legs and get a feel for how the stock market works prior to investing large sums of money and risking a big financial loss. These particular stocks cost literally pennies or small dollar amounts and typically only fluctuate fractions of a cent on any given day, making them extremely safe for those just starting out.

Once you get the hang of it and can better judge the market trends, you can comfortably move on to more complicated and adventurous areas of the market. It is like removing the training wheels from your bicycle or entering the freeway the first time at an hour of the day when there is no traffic to contend with.

Be aware that, just like you may fall off your bike once or twice and end up with some scrapes and bruises, you may lose money in an investment here and there.

This is very typical, and investing in the stock market is a lot like gambling. In poker, you cannot expect to win every hand, and the same is true in the world of investments.

Learning to watch the market trends, though, is similar to watching other cars as you join traffic and determining the correct speed and proximity to other cars for optimal safety. Such diligent study can help you improve your statistics drastically in a short time.

Chapter 2:

Stock Market Trends

(http://en.wikipedia.org/wiki/Market_trend)
Understanding stock market trends can make your job of earning money in the market much simpler. In contrast, if you know little or nothing about these trends can cause serious loss.

BULLS AND BEARS

As you dig deeper into the market and learn more about the way it functions, you will begin to hear certain terms about marketing trends that seem to be repeated over and over again. Market trends are variable and volatile, both on a daily basis and over extended periods of time. In the past, for example, the United States has had devastating stock market crashes, but due to the freedom of a capitalist society, the American economy has always eventually rebound.

What does it mean for the market or a particular stock to rebound? Assuming that the value of a company or its stock has plummeted to a level that seem unrecoverable, leaving it practically worthless, it may feel as though that company is in danger of bankruptcy and falling off the scope of the free trade markets altogether. All of a sudden, however, the founder of that company may introduce a new product over which consumers go wild. Everyone wants one, and this product may be in short supply upon its introduction, causing a race to the department store shelves.

When such a move occurs, the law of supply and demand will take over, making the company valuable once again. The stock price for that company's shares will recover, and the resulting gain in value would be considered a rebound – a return to the original status (or better) prior to the devastating loss.

The market trends either up or down, and there are specific references to strong changes in the market values that you may frequently hear. If several different areas of the market are in a steep downward slide, with values dropping rapidly (perhaps even ten or twenty percent in a few days), it is referred to as a bear market. You can remember this reference as though you are in the extremely dangerous position of being chased by a bear – if you are in possession of several stocks or other commodities worth a goodly sum, you have a serious chance of losing a great deal of value that could translate to a loss of net worth should you choose to sell, and it can be a similar, very dangerous situation.

Your best bet in these cases is to either sell before prices drop below your original purchase price or to hold onto the shares until the market rebounds.

However, when the bear market reaches a low point, it can be an ideal time to get into the game, as it is rare for prices to drop below this point.

Then, if you patiently await the recovery or rebound of the market, you can make a great deal of money from a bear market. These options will be discussed in more depth in later chapters.

At the same time, a bull market is a strong general upward trend for many stocks. You might compare this to the running of the bulls in Pamplona, Spain, every year. You are safer if you are indoors when the running occurs, and by the same token, if you own stock during a bull market, you are in a prime position to increase your net worth and sell your shares, making a great deal of money. This is another idea will be further explored in greater detail further on in this e-book.

THE MARKET OUTLOOK

By taking note of various changes in the status of different available stock options, you will learn how to spot early market trends, giving you a clue to the future of a particular commodity, and this can only add to your chances for profitability.

STOCK MARKET PREDICTION

(http://en.wikipedia.org/wiki/Stock_market_prediction) is a big part of the game when working in the stock market, since you can never be completely certain in what direction the market will swing at any given time.

However, you can make an educated guess, much the same way a meteorologist forecasts the weather. While he or she is not right 100% of the time, the forecast is usually quite close to the actual outcome of the weather because the meteorologist is a scientist who has studied weather trends and can pick out details that assist in making that educated guess.

With a little time and seasoning, you can attain the same level of experience and intuition within the stock market.

Once you have become more comfortable functioning in the same world as the stockbrokers and day traders, and you feel confident (or at least less nervous or awkward) making such important financial decisions, **you may decide to make your move toward the Foreign Exchange Market (more commonly known as Forex),** and the goal of this book is to prepare you to operate within the boundaries of this more complex entity.

Next, we will discuss some of the properties of Forex and how much more complex this stock market entity can be than a standard domestic market.

THE FOREIGN EXCHANGE MARKET IS INCREDIBLY VOLATILE, AND THERE ARE A LOT MORE FACTORS TO CONSIDER WHEN PLACING AN ORDER ON THIS MARKET THAN ON A DOMESTIC MARKET.

The following chapter is an introduction to the exciting and somewhat scary world of the Foreign Exchange Market, or Forex.

INTRODUCTION TO FOREX VIDEO (YOUTUBE)
Learn the basics on online currency trading with this 8 minute video. Forex is one of the largest financial markets in the world - trading over 5.3 trillion in daily volume.
https://www.youtube.com/watch?v=h68UkEyC8Ww

Chapter 3:

An Introduction to Forex

Forex is the nickname for the Foreign Exchange Market. In the United States, there are several branches of the stock market, each with their own name. For instance, some stocks trade on the Dow Jones, others on NASDAQ. Of course, all stock market transactions in the United States take place on the New York Stock Exchange (NYSE). In other countries the same is true.

There may be one or more distinct markets. However, international trade takes place on the market termed the Foreign Exchange Market, or Forex. Several countries across the world in almost every time zone participate in trade on Forex, with multiple currencies being utilized and stocks and commodities from all participating countries being offered for trade.

Because there are so many nations and time zones involved, Forex does not function as a "business day" entity like most domestic stock markets.

IT REMAINS OPEN FOR TRADE 24 HOURS A DAY, 5 DAYS A WEEK.

The forex market is open almost all of the time! It opens on Sunday night around 21:00 GMT and closes on Friday afternoon around 21:00 GMT.

Forex traders can initiate trades at any time between Sunday and Friday.

According to GMT, for instance, forex trading hours move around the world like this: available in New York between 01:00 pm – 10:00 pm GMT; at 10:00 pm GMT Sydney comes online; Tokyo opens at 00:00 am and closes at 9:00 am GMT; and to complete the loop, London opens at 8:00 am and closes at 05:00 pm GMT.
Of course, these additional hours increase the risk factor intensely for those of us who are human and obviously cannot monitor our investments 24 hours a day.

This means that the value of your holdings could potentially plummet overnight, while you sleep, because other countries are still trading while you are in a dream world. Again, it is like a car – there are many moving pieces under the hood, and just because you cannot see them does not mean they are not functioning.

This is one reason for several safety options, like limit orders, which we will discuss later. This is also why it is strongly recommended that your first attempts to make money on the stock market are not transactions that take place within the Foreign Exchange Market but on a standard nine-to-five domestic trading market.

In our car analogy, this would be comparable to having asked someone who has never driven or even changed the oil in a car to rebuild the engine.

FOREX FUNCTIONALITY

While the functionality of Forex is the same as a domestic stock exchange, the commodities and prices are more volatile, and there are additional factors to take into considerations besides the typical risks associated with a domestic market. You will have to contend with not only the value of your stocks and your currency, but also the foreign currencies involved in any trades or exchanges on Forex, as well as the inconsistencies of values of particular goods and services across international borders.

It is like driving a car with a standard transmission as opposed to an automatic.

On the domestic front, the work is mostly done for you, and all you have to do is navigate, much like an automatic transmission. However, shifting gears is quite similar to having to constantly take part in the currency conversion. It can be distracting, and it certainly complicates the act of driving.

Because the financial situation of many countries is not as secure as that of the United States, this can pose a formidable problem in determining where to invest your money and what to expect next in the international market. Knowing what countries and currencies are involved in Forex can assist you by allowing you to more closely monitor the financial situation in the nations with which you will be interacting.

THE HISTORY OF FOREX

When foreign trade began, it was not an international trade market. It was borne out of the Bretton Woods agreement in 1944, which set forth that foreign currencies would be fixed against the dollar, which was valued at $35 per ounce of gold. This precedent was first put into practice in 1967, when a bank in Chicago refused to fund a loan to a professor in sterling pound. Of course, his intention was to sell the currency, which he felt was priced too high against the dollar, then buy it back later when the value had declined, turning a quick profit.

After 1971, when the dollar was no longer convertible to gold and the domestic market was stronger, the Bretton Woods agreement was abandoned, and the currency conversion process became more variable.

This allowed for a stronger backing in the foreign markets, and the United States and Europe began a strong trade relationship. In the 1980s, the market hours and usage was extended through the use of computers and technology to include the Asian time zones as well. At this time, foreign exchange equaled about $70 billion a day.

Today, about twenty years later, the trade level has skyrocketed, with trade equaling close to $5.3 trillion daily.

Originally, trading across international lines was more difficult, with several different currencies involved across Europe. Though the major players in the European market were deeply involved in and veterans of international trade by the time other markets joined in, there were more currencies to keep track of – the franc, the pound, the lira, and many more – than was reasonable.

With the birth of the European Union in 1992, the wheels were set in motion to create a single currency that would be used across most of Europe, and the Euro was finally established and put into circulation in 1999.

GO HERE FOR MORE INFORMATION
History of the Forex
http://www.investopedia.com/walkthrough/forex/beginner/level2/history.aspx

FOREX TODAY

While some countries have still not accepted the currency as their own (such as Britain, who still uses the sterling pound), the process of currency conversion has been simplified without the large number of various currencies that were previously dealt with. Instead of dozens of currencies, the main countries trade in five – U.S. dollars,

Australian dollars, British pounds sterling, the Euro, and the Japanese Yen.
Today, the Foreign Exchange Market is international and worldwide.

The market is open 24 hours a day, 5 days a week, to accommodate all of the time zones for all of the major players. These now include most of Europe, the United States, and Asian markets, especially Japan. Even Australia has joined the international trading markets, and since such nations are halfway around the world from some of the other top players, time zones obviously must be taken into consideration.

Another completely separate but perhaps more important concern with trading in Forex is understanding how trade works in multiple currencies.

How can you compare the value of a stock across international lines if the values are expressed in two separate, non-equivalent currencies? And how do you measure gains and losses when conversion rate is constantly changing?

Chapter 4:

Understanding Currency Conversion

When you begin trading on Forex, you have to learn how to convert currencies and note the difference in values, as well as how currencies are exchanged between international lines. This means studying not only domestic market trends and currency values, but also those of foreign markets.

(Understanding the Spread in Retail Currency Exchange Rates
http://www.investopedia.com/articles/forex/090914/understanding-spread-retail-currency-exchange-rates.asp)

WORKING WITH MULTIPLE CURRENCIES

Since Forex is the Foreign Exchange Market, you obviously cannot expect everyone within the market to trade in U.S. dollars (and why not, you might ask? – but remember that not everyone covets the U.S. dollar). With so many variables and volatile currencies being exchanged, how can you know a good buy or sell when you see one without complete awareness of the value of foreign currency?

The first step is to find a source that will give you a basic idea of the current exchange rate between your domestic currency and the foreign currency in question. You should do this as a base listing for any currency that with which you might become involved. Of course, this will not be consistent down to the cent or fraction of a particular currency throughout an entire business day, but at least you will have your starting point from which to begin, almost like North on a compass. Such sources can be found all over the Internet, as well as through many brokers, both on line and in person.

CURRENCY EXPRESSION

It is also good to understand the means by which the currency conversion is expressed. The comparison is usually made in a ratio known as the cross-rate. In this configuration, the two currencies are listed in an XXX/YYY ratio, with the XXX position referred to as the base currency.

The base currency is usually expressed as a whole number, while the YYY position is expressed as the decimal that most closely matches the based currency rate. It is sort of like making reference to miles per gallon or rotations per minute on a car – a direct comparison of one to the other in the form of a ratio.

The smallest fraction, or decimal, in which a currency can be traded, is called a pip and this is usually the degree to which a cross-rate is expressed. For example, if the British pound sterling can be traded in thousandths, the currency will be expressed to the third decimal place.

The U.S. dollar is often expressed to the hundredth of a cent (the fourth decimal place). In one cross-rate expression example, one U.S. dollar may be equivalent to 117.456 Japanese yen. This ratio would be expressed as 1.000/117.456. The base currency is almost always expressed as a single unit (as in one dollar as opposed to ten dollars), and frequently that unit of measurement is the U.S. dollar. Since the whole number value (or big figure, as it is referred to) of the secondary currency, or the currency in the YYY position in terms of conversion changes so infrequently, often only the decimal portion of the number is mentioned in the Foreign Exchange Market.

Therefore, in the ratio above, you may hear that the yen is trading at .456, with no mention at all of the 117 whole yen that is shown in the ratio. This is because the exchange rate may vary from 117.456 to 117.423, but not to 119.024.

Experiencing a change in the big figure – the whole number ahead of the decimal – unless it was only because the number was already within a few thousandths, would represent much too large a shift in value for a single trading period and would be a rare occurrence that could cause the entire market to make a drastic swing in one direction or the other.

The most common currencies found in Forex are the U.S. dollar, the British pound sterling, the Euro, the Japanese yen, and the Australian dollar. In the past, there would have been many more currencies to keep track of (such as the franc, the lira, or the Deutschmark). However, with the consolidation of most of the European market trading on Forex to the Euro, many currencies have been eliminated, making trade on Forex for other lands less complicated.

If you purchase a commodity in a particular currency, and that currency's value falls against the U.S. dollar, you can actually make money by selling that same commodity in dollars. The same is true in reverse should the value of a foreign currency increase against a U.S. dollar. Of course, you can only take advantage of such a situation should the commodity be traded in both currencies and both markets in question. We will discuss this process, as well as other ways to take advantage of the Foreign Exchange Market (like arbitrage) in more depth in future chapters. Once you are able to discern a base value of each particular currency and its conversion rate against others traded on Forex, you will be able to more closely monitor the change in currency conversion, including its inconsistency and volatility.

Such ideas will not seem so "foreign", and you will be caught up and knowledgeable right along with the pros. Then, you will need to learn how to read, understand, and ultimately interpret additional market trends.

FOREX TRENDING
(Forex: Identifying Trending And Range-Bound Currencies http://www.investopedia.com/articles/forex/05/062205.asp)

Following charts, listening to the advice of market analysts and chartists, and learning to make educated predictions yourself will help you keep track of various marketing trends.

The next chapter will explain more about using the statistics that are published to forecast the next move on the stock market.

Will it be a clear, calm day with little activity, or is there a storm brewing with winds of change and uncertainty? How can you tell what will happen with your holdings the following day or even further into the future?

Simply learning to read market trends can remove a lot of natural apprehension and uncertainty for beginning traders. In fact, sometimes the best first step to entering the market is to watch shows about it or read the financial sections of the newspaper that detail the trends and expected outcomes.

The following chapter will explain more about how to interpret the statistics and basic trends.

Chapter 5:

Understanding Statistics

You have now become somewhat familiar with how the stock market works, and you understand to a point what is involved in trading on the Foreign Exchange Market. Now, you would like to know how to gauge market trends in order to profit from your business ventures on the open market. We are no longer discussing penny stocks and playground games. You want the real goods.

The name of the game is statistics, and the first rule is that you must be aware there is no such thing as a sure thing on the stock market. While you can never be 100% sure at any given time of the next move that will be made on the market as a whole, being able to read statistics and interpret them will place you ahead of the pack in regards to "guessing" what will happen next.

Investing is a lot like gambling. If you can keep track of the cards that have already been played, you are more informed, statistically, regarding what is likely to be dealt next, meaning you can place abet with greater insight than someone who has no clue what has already been played. With the open market, if you have information as to what has already occurred over the past few days, months, or even years, you are again placed in a better position to more logically conclude what will happen next. You simply learn the pattern and follow it to the end, reaping the financial rewards.

CHARTS AND CHARTISTS

Wait, did you think you were going to have to research and map out the markets past all by yourself? Of course not! There are people who get paid to do that sort of work.

They monitor the market hourly, daily, weekly, monthly, and yearly so that they can provide big-time traders with the same knowledge mentioned before. The more an investment company knows about the market, the more money they can make. The same is true for stockbrokers.

They make money when you make money, and they want to do the best they can to make sure that you make intelligent decisions.

The best part of this is that you have access to the same information as these VIP clients. Chartists, who are essentially market analysts that publish their findings in easy to read charts, produce what is referred to as a candlestick chart.

These charts are basically a combination of a line graph and a bar graph that show the trend of various stocks, indexes, or other interests over a specified period of time. Therefore, you can easily determine if the commodity is on an uptrend or if it is taking a downturn, when the last major change occurred, and how long it is predicted that the stock or bond will continue on the current path.

You can actually find information on most commodities and their market trends for years in the past, and some even all the way back to their introduction to the open market.

Using this information can help you decide whether it is a good idea to buy or sell the stocks or securities in which you have interest, or if it is better to hold off for a peak in the market trend.

UNDERSTANDING MARKET TRENDS
(Factors That Shape Market Trends http://www.investopedia.com/articles/trading/09/what-factors-create-trends.asp)

Understandably, as economies vary, the value of various commodities can change. This is because, when an economy is strong and flourishing, a nation is wealthier and has more purchasing power. Along with that power comes a higher value for the items purchased. In other words, if people have more money to spend and are spending a greater amount of that money at Walmart stores, the value of stock at Walmart is going to multiply at a considerable rate.

Therefore, stockholders become wealthier in terms of assets, simply because the shoppers are driving the market with their purchasing power. When stockholders are wealthy, and the value of their holdings is on the rise, they continue to purchase stock, which again, pumps the economy.

A strong upward trend in the stock market is an excellent sign for any economy.

However, there are also things that affect the market in a negative fashion, causing stock values to plummet. For example, warfare rarely has a positive effect on the stock market. On September 11, 2001, when terrorists attacked the World Trade Center in New York City, the economy of the United States took a huge dive, and the nation was threatened with a depression. Some analysts were sure that it would never properly recover.

The same thing typically happens any time there is an attack or act of war within a nation.

However, the critics proved to be wrong, and the United States proceeded to rebound, or recover from a bad downtrend, in a strong manner.

This quick recovery occurred mostly because the people of the United States continued to push and spend, forcing money and wealth back into the economy. In watching the reaction of the stock market, you can learn to read trends based on world events.

Oil prices commonly affect the stock market, as well. Especially on the Foreign Exchange Market, you will find trends vary depending on many current events. You will also note that, over time, the principle value (or face value) of a currency may purposely be revised by a nation in terms of currency conversion. This is referred to as devaluation, which will be discussed in greater detail in the following chapter.

Chapter 6:

Forex Volatility and Market Expectation

Volatility, or the tendency for fluctuation that can affect your earnings within the stock market, is typical within a domestic market but even more evident and much stronger on the Foreign Exchange Market.

What factors affect the value of currency on Forex, and is there any way to control this?

DEVALUATION AND REVALUATION

As mentioned in the previous chapter, devaluation refers to the purposeful decline in value of a currency in relation to other currencies as charged by a government entity.

For example, if the U. S. dollar is worth ten units of a foreign currency that is then devalued by ten percent, the U. S. dollar is now equivalent to only nine units of the foreign currency.

This makes any items purchased in the foreign currency more expensive for those trading in U. S. dollars, as the exchange rate is lowered. It also makes items in the foreign country less expensive to trade in U. S. dollars.

An opposite change in value can also occur, raising the value of the foreign currency. This is referred to as revaluation.

While it may seem that purposely adjusting the value of a nation's currency is "cheating", or taking an unfair advantage by making foreign products cheaper to purchase and increasing the value of exports, there are regulations in place to prevent the manipulation of exchange rates for such purposes.

The charter of the IMF (International Monetary Fund) assists in prohibiting such occurrences and enforcing the policy.

(AN INTRODUCTION TO THE INTERNATIONAL MONETARY FUND (IMF) http://www.investopedia.com/articles/03/030703.asp)

There are ways in which you can take advantage of devaluation and revaluation, which will be discussed later on. However, what happens when the value of a foreign currency changes due to market fluctuation rather than purposeful reductions or increases by a federal government or federal bank?

What effect do appreciation and depreciation have on the stock market?

APPRECIATION AND DEPRECIATION

Depreciation can be easily related to the life of a car. As soon as you drive a new car off the lot, the value is almost cut in half. This is extreme depreciation. However, over the next few years, the car continues to lose value at a more gradual pace. This is considered to be depreciation as well.

Currency appreciation and depreciation are changes in the value of the currency that are driven by market forces rather than by government mandate. For example, in an attempt to repay certain loans, in 1998 the Central Bank of Russia announced the coming devaluation of the ruble.

The exchange rate, which was currently six rubles per U.S. dollar, would over a period of time change to 9.5 rubles per dollar, effectively a depreciation of 34%.

However, prior to the change, there was a widespread panic within the former Communist nation, and the value of the ruble dropped due to many people in Russia opting to trade in their securities prior to maturity. In a single day, following the announcement, the Russian ruble was depreciated by an amazing 25%.

The same sort of crisis occurred in the 1920's with the crash of the U.S. stock market. In that time, a nationwide panic set in, and people rushed to the banks to withdraw cash that was not available or to trade in securities and stock options that were not matured. In running to the bank, people actually caused the crash rather than escaped it.

On the flip side of the coin, too fast of an appreciation sets up a country for inflation, or an increase in the retail value of products sold to the public based on currency valuation. While inflation is bound to occur, it can be minimally tempered through the use of the currency valuation.

Appreciation can be related to a vehicle as well. Often, men enjoy taking old cars and restoring them to their original beauty. In doing so; they drastically increase the value of the vehicle or appreciate it.

The ever changing rates of currency conversion and volatility of the market create an inherent market risk, or a day to day potential to experience loss due to fluctuation in securities prices. There is no way to diversify this type of risk, as it is always going to affect investment to a certain degree.

However, some risk can be offset by particular types of investments or ways of investing that are more secure or protected.
We will take a look at long and short positions, short selling, stop orders, and other ways to protect your investments from drastic loss in

additional chapters. These options include the ability to preset your purchase or sell price for a specific commodity, as well as using various predetermine order levels to place orders and complete transactions.

Of course, do not delude yourself into thinking that you can rid yourself of all possible risk factors on the market. There is always a cloud hanging over your head waiting to burst, and all it takes is one little pinprick. You must always exercise caution, though the idea of playing the stock market entails danger and excitement inherently.

The next chapter will help you get a grasp on reality and what is involved in balancing your risk factor with a grounding in reality; your ego with your id.

Chapter 7:

Aspects of The Trade

You are now versed in the functionality of the stock market and have decided that you are willing to accept the risk factors involved. However, you want to know everything you can about balancing that risk with intelligent investment options. How can you be sure that the risks you take are more likely to be rewarding in the long run than destructive?

LONG AND SHORT

One of the most important parts of making money on the stock market is to determine your position.

- The long position is basically the purchasing position – you are about to take on a long-term commitment for ownership of some stock, security, or other traded commodity.

- The short position, by contrast, is the selling position – you are shortly going to dispose of the same sort of ownership and any responsibility toward it.

The best time to take up the long position is when stock prices are low. This will get you into the market at a reasonable price and increase your chances for profitability as new offerings go up in price and older investment options recover or rebound. In fact, as others take the long position and purchase at the same time you do, this will actually drive the value of securities up through the standard rule of supply and demand, causing the beginning of what could be a bull market.

You may equate this with the end of the month at a car dealership. The prices tend to drop on any cars left on the lot for sale, and the dealer is more often willing to bargain because he or she wants less inventory on the lot.

Likewise, when stock prices are low, some will panic and dump all of their holdings at these low prices, thinking that their shares will never recover the value. This can only be of assistance to you.

When prices are high, it is likely time to turn around and sell your shares to bring in a profit, not losing anything on unrealized gain (profit that cannot be counted in liquid assets or cash because it is still invested in a volatile stock option).

You should never sell for a price that is below your cost, as this brings negative equity and loss of funds. You should always sell for the greatest amount of profit that you feel is safe.

In other words, if you buy a security at fifteen dollars per share, and it quickly rises to twenty-five dollars per share, you may very well feel that it could hit thirty dollars per share within a week. However, you must determine if you are willing to risk losing your already secured earnings of ten dollars per share to wait that long, should the price actually fall, so you may decide to sell at the current high price.

MARKET-MAKERS AND SELLING SHORT

What if the stock values are up incredibly high, but you did not get in on that particular commodity and own no shares?

Your first step should be to visit a market-maker or to make a deal with a broker for a short sell. A market-maker is literally a stockbroker who purchases keeps a certain amount of shares of several securities or stocks on hand, which are purchased during a time when the market rates are low.

The firm will then turn around and sell those shares to an individual at that low price, regardless of the market rate, in effect making its own market (thus the name). The individual who purchases from the firm can immediately sell the commodities on the open market at market rate (which is higher), making an incredible amount of profit in a short period of time.

A short sell is another option for a quick profit. In this scenario, you will borrow a particular number of shares from a stockbroker to sell when the market value is high. Your job is to then wait for the stock price to go down, purchase the same quantity of stock, and return the holdings to the broker, keeping the profit from the sale, minus the broker fees.

The way that a car dealer works with trade-ins is very similar. They will purchase the car from you at a very low price, then turn around and sell it on the lot for a high profit margin.

One of the most positive aspects of a short sell is that you never actually take possession of the stock, meaning that you are never in a position to lose money. Because you have sold shares for a high price, you have already profited, and in the worst-case scenario, the particular stocks will not drop in price.

Rather than return the stocks to the broker from whom they were borrowed, you can simply pay back the amount for which they were originally purchased, along with the premium.

How can you be sure that you will not overshoot the best price options or miss a good rate because you are unavailable to place a buy order or sell order with your broker? Is there a way to set limits on your trades?

Next, we will discuss ways to protect your investments and limit your risk factors.

Chapter 8:

Risk Management

One of the most important aspects of protecting your investments is balancing your risks with reassurances. There are several ways to do this, and we will discuss those in this chapter.

LIMIT ORDERS AND BALANCING RISKS

(STOP-LOSS ORDER
http://www.investopedia.com/terms/s/stop-lossorder.asp)

A limit order is a standing amount at which you have agreed to buy or sell a particular security or other commodity. For instance, you have designated to your stockbroker that you will not sell X Security until its value reaches a minimum value of Y dollars. At the same time, you will not purchase the same X Security if it exceeds a value of Z. Setting limits for the price you pay for a particular security, as well as the price you will accept to sell it, protects you and your investment in several ways.

First of all, you are maximizing your gains, but mostly, you are avoiding loss. Any loss that occurs with limit orders will always be unrealized loss, or a loss that is not measurable in liquid assets or cash. In other words, until you sell the stock and reap the net loss, it will not affect your net worth. Since you have set a limit that does not allow your commodities to be sold for less than the original cost, you cannot possibly have a loss in your net worth. At the same time, you are also assuring at least a certain amount of profit by setting your sell point high enough to reap that particular profit.

Another way to protect your assets is to hedge. This means that you create and sell a futures contract stating that, when your shares reach a certain value in the future, you will sell your holdings at this predetermined price. When that price is reached, the order will be processed and the transaction completed.

Of course, if you ever change your mind about a limit that you have set, you can place a stop order with your broker, which designates that you no longer wish to trade at the specified dollar amount.

You can also buy on margin. This is very similar to short selling, but instead of borrowing stocks to sell, you are essentially borrowing money to purchase stocks on your own when the market value is down. Then, when the value of the securities you have purchased rises and you are able to sell for a profit, you repay the loan and keep the excess from the sell, minus the broker fees.

Of course, all dealings with a stockbroker incur a premium, or fee for services rendered, and it is nearly impossible to trade without a broker or broker service. However, online services are often less expensive than live agents, but you can research to determine what your best option is.

HOW DO I HANDLE A WHIPSAW?

No, we are not referring to anything in the garage, the bedroom, or a country band. A whipsaw is market trend that defies the odds. It can be thought of as the "fender bender". Despite how careful you are as you learn to drive a car and become coordinated, sometimes you cannot do anything to avoid being rear-ended.

Whipsaw is a term for what happens when everything points toward a specific direction in market trend, causing you to buy (if it looks as though prices are going to rise) or sell (if it seems they are about to fall), then the opposite effect occurs.

For example, if you purchase a security at five dollars per share because the stock seems to have fallen as far as it can go and appears to be starting an upward trend, then unexpectedly, the stock plummets to one dollar per share, this is considered a whipsaw effect.

If this happens to you, as it surely will if you play the market long enough, the best thing to do is wait it out. The stock will do one of two things – it will either dissolve entirely, and the company will go bankrupt (this is what you do not want to happen), or it will rebound, and you can opt to wait for a chance to turn a profit or you can get out as soon as the purchase rate is reached.

Whipsaws are not the end of the world, and no one can expect to gain with every stock market purchase.

However, if you find that you are involved in several of these instances, you should seriously reconsider your investment options. You may be reading the signs incorrectly, or you could be picking bad stocks. You should seek advice for any future investments you expect to make prior to purchasing any further stocks or securities. Another way to overturn a bad investment like this is to proceed with an offset transaction – a purchase or sell that offsets the loss of a previous transaction.

You could either purchase additional stock in the same company at the lower price if you expect it to recover, or you can opt for another hot commodity that is about to explode in price, either of which will help you offset your loss.

You could also sell shares of a security in which you have a large amount of unrealized gain – gain that cannot be measured in liquid assets or cash due to increase in value of stock and security holdings – in order to replace the lost cash value.

All of these are viable options to recover a loss, but waiting for the share value to rebound is always the first choice. It avoids the loss of funds already invested, retains the option to pursue profit, and reduces the risk of further investment into the market.

As you grow and learn about these various options, you will need to feel more comfortable when surrounded by financial gurus and geeks who speak what sounds like gibberish, muttering words you have never heard left and right.

The following chapter will take you through some of the meanings of the major "buzz" words used in the stock market and the international financial district.

Chapter 9:

Buzz Words

Now that you know a little more about the stock market, and you have decided to try your hand at investment, you should be more concerned with understanding the jargon you will hear on the trading room floor.

Although you probably will not find yourself amid a group of screaming stockbrokers on Wall Street (and these days, most of the trading is done by computer anyway), knowing that learning to talk the talk is part of walking the walk.

MARGINS, SPREADS, AND OTHER CONDIMENTS

Okay, so it is margins, not margarines, but it sounds very similar. In order to understand the stock market, especially on Forex, you need to speak not a language meant for common communication, but the language of trade. For instance, when you think of a margin, for many this means a variable – like the "margin of error" in a statistic.

However, in trade, it refers to the sum of money borrowed from a broker in order to purchase stocks when the market is on a downtrend. Then, when the value begins its next upswing, you sell the stock at the higher price, pay back the margin (along with the premium accrued), and retain the profit.

When you buy on margin, the money lent by the stockbroker is referred to as a margin account. The margin account is provisional based on the value of the stock.

Occasionally, if the value of the stocks purchased should drop too low for the safety margin set forth by the broker, the agent will request that more money be deposited into the margin account to make up for loss. This is referred to as a margin call.

In some trades, the market value does not come into play. For instance, a forward trade is set up between two individuals or two companies outside the open market. It involves a process of negotiation and an eventual compromise in price. There is usually a bid made – the offer to buy a commodity at a certain price – and an asking price or offer – the price for which the other business entity is willing to sell the securities or other holdings.

The difference between these two purchase numbers is referred to as the spread.
If the spread cannot be narrowed and eventually closed, no deal can be made.

This agreed-upon price is called the forward price, and all details involved in the trade process when this type of transaction takes place are detailed in a contract and referred to as forward points.

Usually, the forward price is outlined as available for a particular date, and should the transaction not be completed on this date (referred to as the transaction date), then the trade must be renegotiated.

JOBBERS, YARDS, AND OTHER "BRIT" TERMS

One of the major foreign markets that Americans trading on Forex will encounter is that of the British. While several other terms relating to the stock market will be similar because of the common language, there are some specific terms that are very different in the British trading vocabulary.

For example, in the United States, stockbrokers who hold onto securities purchased at low prices for the purpose of selling them to clients in a higher priced market (so that the client can turn around and resell them for the profit on the open market) are called market-makers. However, in Britain, this type of investor is simply referred to as a "jobber".

ANOTHER TERM YOU WILL WANT TO BE FAMILIAR WITH IS "YARD"

This does not refer to a green patch of land, a measurement in inches, or even 36 of something.

The term is used in reference to quantity of currency rather than value and is equivalent to one million units of the currency in question. In other words, you can have a yard of dollars or a yard of yen, and though it is the same quantity of bills, coins, or whatever physical currency is used, it is not necessarily equivalent in value. In Britain, they do not use the Euro, and they do not use the U.S. dollar.

They have chosen to still use the pound sterling, a currency that has been used in the country for hundreds of years. However, Britain is currently on a path to make the conversion to the Euro within the next five years.

OPEN AND SHUT

In the stock market, there are various types of orders that can be placed to help protect you from making a bad investment or to limit the amount you pay for a certain security or other commodity. For instance, if you have made a bad investment and do not want to reinvest in a particular security, you should sell all shares of that stock, regardless of taking on a small loss.

This action is referred to as closing a position. On the contrary, if you are doing well with your investment, you might participate in a rollover, simply reinvesting any earnings in additional shares of the stock or security.

An open order is exactly what it sounds like, meaning that the order remains pending until it is either executed by your stockbroker or canceled by you as the client. A stop order would cancel any pending orders you have placed with your stockbroker. You also have options like One Cancels the Other Orders.

These allow you to have interest in several commodities, leaving orders with your stockbroker to buy all of them, should they drop to a certain price. Then, should one of those reach this preset low price, your stockbroker will follow your direction and invest your money in that particular security, followed by a cancellation of all additional orders.

When a broker gives you an estimate on the price for a particular stock or commodity, it is considered a quote. A quote is never completely accurate and is usually referred to as a spot price, as the value of a security can change within a few seconds. However, it is as close to accurate as can be expected.

When you put in an order, the broker then processes the fill, or completion, of that order. The actual value at which the trade is completed is called the fill price. The completion of a trade or purchase, referred to as a settlement, can also be called the execution of a transaction or realization of an order. As you see, there are a lot of terms to take into consideration, and we have not even begun to consider terms used in some of the tougher areas of the market.

Next, we will consider some specialized, more complex trading options that you can use on Forex to take advantage of the volatility of the market and the constantly varying exchange rates.

Chapter 10:

Expert Trading Options

After spending a lot of time buying and trading on both domestic and foreign markets, you will find that the process becomes easier and almost intuitive. You no longer have to work so hard to determine currency conversion or find the next big explosive commodity. It will be like second nature for you.

What, then, becomes the next big challenge for someone trading on the open market? What keeps things from becoming monotonous and boring? First of all, there is always something new and different happening on the Foreign Exchange Market. Remember, it operates 24 hours a day, and you never know what you will find when you wake up in the morning. However, there are various ways that you can take advantage of the variance in currency conversion and a lag in time between markets that can affect trading values.

ARBITRAGE

There are some commodities that are traded in multiple currencies on multiple markets on Forex. Although computers have made worldwide communication almost lightning fast these days, all of these markets can trade together with fairly equivalent values for the securities shared across currencies.

However, the system is not perfect, and the value may rise or fall in one country and currency prior to the same change in value reaching across another border.

Seasoned traders have learned to take advantage of this lag in the market trending by using a process called arbitrage.

In this transaction, you purchase the particular stock or security on the market with the lower price while simultaneously selling the same in a market where the value is higher.

The process is a bit complex, so we will use an example. Let's say that one U.S. dollar is equivalent to .5 British pounds, meaning that everything is going to be twice as expensive in British pounds.

Now, let's take a look at the price of a stock that is traded on both markets. If they were equivalent, then the stock would trade for two dollars in the United States and one pound in Britain. However, if something happens and the stock value drops in Britain, it is six hours ahead of the United States, and this drop may not hit the American market immediately.

If the value of the stock drops in Britain to .8 pounds, the purchase price is now below that of the price in dollars due to the currency conversion. In this case, arbitrage would take place when you bought shares of the stock in on the British market in pounds and sold it on the U.S. market in dollars, benefiting by the slow communication of the fall in value of the stock. In effect, you will make $.40 per stock.

VOLATILITY OF CURRENCY CONVERSION

Another way to take advantage of the ever-shifting value of each individual currency is to trade based on the changing rates. What exactly does this involve?

You must closely watch the changing conversion rates. When a currency conversion rate changes drastically, it is time to make a move. This is very similar to arbitrage, but the area is much riskier due to high volatility.

For instance, if you have purchased a stock in the scenario above on the U.S. market for two dollars a share, and suddenly the British pound gains value, dropping to a conversion of only half a pound for every two dollars, you would want to sell your shares on the British market because the value of a pound is higher and now has greater purchasing power.

One piece of advice to keep in mind, though, is that it is best to immediately dispose of all liquid assets in foreign currency, usually in the same day. This is referred to as tomorrow next because it takes two to three business days for foreign currency to be delivered, and by exchanging the currency for value in stocks on the same business day, you avoid having to take delivery of the currency altogether.

Chapter 11:
Other Trading Options

Besides the expert options described above, there are other nontraditional ways to make money on the stock market. In considering these options, however, you should consider making a career of trading stocks and securities. Some types of trading are simply not for the faint of heart, and that means you must have complete motivation and an adventurous spirit to take part in these areas of the market. The chances of taking a giant hit and experiencing a great loss are multiplied.

DAY TRADING
(**AN INTRODUCTION TO DAY TRADING**
http://www.investopedia.com/articles/trading/05/011705.asp)

Day traders take on some of the greatest market risk of all. Because day traders work with investments that change drastically within hours, they are by nature playing in the lion's den. These stocks are extremely volatile, and for most, day trading is a quick way to lose a great deal of money.

It is difficult to make a great deal of cash in this manner, and it is even more difficult to forecast the outcome of these day trade stock options. You cannot be certain of the overnight position (the net value at which a stockbroker or day trader will open the following morning).

And in Forex, there is little room for day trading, as the market never shuts down during the workweek. In these cases, the day trader has to set a time limit for him- or herself to get out, selling all shares, so that he or she can sleep soundly while the world spins round and start the next day fresh.

Day trading is very dangerous and is not recommended to newcomers. In fact, it is not really recommended at all, and most people who partake of this volatile part of the industry are extremely seasoned in trading on the open market, do not consider the risk factors carefully enough prior to entering this branch of the market, or have enough money that they simply wish to try this form of investment and do not care if they lose a goodly sum.

SECONDARY MARKETS

Secondary markets are interesting in that they are created by the government to help redistribute money that is used for loans. Fannie Mae and Freddie Mac are two of the major corporations from which stocks are purchased on a secondary market.

Here is how it works. When a person purchases a home, he or she requests a loan from the bank, usually for about eighty percent of the cost of the house. This is granted, and the house is purchased by the bank for the individual or family, who begins to pay off the loan to the bank.

Meanwhile, to assure that money is available at that bank for the next person who needs a mortgage loan, Fannie Mae or Freddie Mac, two entities originally established by the United States government, will purchase the loan from the bank?

Therefore, the money is returned to the bank for use in the future.

What do these agencies then do with the deficit they have acquired? They sell it. On the secondary market, they break up the loan into shares that are backed by the mortgage itself and sell those shares, recovering the money from investors.

Eventually, those securities mature, probably about the same time that the original loan is paid off to the bank, and the investors reap the benefits of their investment with the interest earned.

Another way to take advantage of a volatile international stock market is to make a swap. This is the exchange of securities or bonds in order to take advantage of lower interest rates.

For example, if a business entity in Britain is in possession of one security, and another in Japan is in possession of a different security, the two commodities may be beneficially traded or sold to each other in order to save on the interest rates, if

the currently held bond or security is kept at a lower interest rate in the opposing market.
For example, let's say one business is in possession of a bond "A" that is paying out only two percent interest in its current market, and another is holding bonds "B" in its market at three percent interest.

If bond A is actually paying out three percent on the foreign market, and bond B can be cashed in for four percent on the first market, both parties can make more money on a trade of bonds. They can mutually benefit from a sale of the securities to each other due to a gain of more interest.

If that seems confusing, then perhaps a swap is not in your near future.

This is more often processed between businesses on the foreign market rather than individual parties, though with the correct broker, it could be accomplished. However, should you work the deal, you need know little except that you are looking at a higher profit margin than previously, and your broker will take care of the rest.

If you determine that you should have stock options as a business, you will probably decide to hire a fulltime consultant for all your financial needs, including the handling of your share holdings.

In fact, when businesses are large enough and present a strong enough trading presence within the market, especially on Forex, you will find that there are entire departments dedicated to maintenance on the stock options.

Chapter 12:

In Review

After shoveling through piles of information and taking in so much knowledge, you probably feel like you are swimming in terminology and cannot remember just where to begin. The best way to retain knowledge is through repetition, and having a quick reference guide is never a bad idea, either. The following pages are a brief overview of the in depth discussions in this book, allowing you to quickly reference a topic in a bind.

THE BASIC TRADE

A share is a holding of a company that varies in value based on the desire or need for that particular company's goods or services. As a shareholder, your net worth increases and decreases based on taking a short position (selling) when values are high and a long position (buying) when prices are low. As long as the stock or security is in your possession, the change in value is considered unrealized gain or loss because you cannot measure it in liquid assets (cash).

When most commodities traded on the market are on a strong upward trend for a period of time, this is referred to as a bull market. Should value take a sharp downward swing and continue on that path, it is called a bear market. If no such trend is recognized, and the value of stocks and securities is fairly even, this is referred to as flat.

THE FOREIGN EXCHANGE MARKET

The Foreign Exchange Market is the stock exchange on which several different countries across several different time zones trade their domestic and international commodities in various currencies. Currency is the denomination or monetary division used in a particular land (such as the U.S. dollar or the Euro).

When multiple currencies are in use, they are typically expressed as a ratio called a cross-rate that shows the amount of a second currency that is equivalent to the first listed. Determining what the equivalent is would be referred to as currency conversion.

Several countries in Europe, which have now consolidated their currencies to agree on the Euro (since 1999) trade on Forex, as it is called for short. Britain, which to this point has opted to continue using the pound sterling, also takes part in international trade, as well as the United States, Japan, and Australia.

Each of these countries utilizes its own currency for standard trading purposes, with options for investment in foreign currencies. Determining whether or not this is worthwhile depends on the currency conversion rate.

The value of a nation's currency is determined by its government and federal bank (the Federal Reserve, better known as the FED, is the federal bank of the United States). Purposeful change in the rate of conversion by a government is referred to as valuation – devaluation is taking value and strength from the currency, and revaluation adds strength and purchase power to the currency.

If the same change to the rate of conversion occurs naturally through events and the volatility of the market, it is then called appreciation and depreciation.

CAREERS IN THE MARKET

Without the assistance of professionals, it is nearly impossible to trade on the open market. Market analysts track trends in the stock market that affect the value of share holdings. They use such information and basic history to help predict the outcome of different aspects of the market in the future.

CHARTISTS

Other individuals, referred to as chartists, create charts and graphs that interpret all the data – various numbers, statistics, percentages, etc. – into an easy to read candlestick chart that tracks the trends of specific commodities on the market.

STOCKBROKER

A stockbroker is an individual or a company that assists you in making your investments. A broker can aid you in making smart financial decisions, helping you track your and place your orders, and following trends in the market.

MARKET-MAKER

A market-maker does the same job as a stockbroker, with the exception that this individual or company retains an investment in a particular variety of securities and bonds that can be sold in short order to a client for a lower price so that the client can make money by immediately selling the same shares at the higher market price.

LOAN BROKER

Other individuals can assist with loans, allowing you to buy on margin. This involves the opposite approach – borrowing money to purchase a stock or security that is at a low market value so that the client can later resell the commodity at a higher price.

PROTECTING YOUR INVESTMENTS

There are several ways to protect your investments. By placing limit orders, you guarantee to the best of your ability that you will not lose money on the market and virtually guarantee at least a minimal profit. However, if you change your mind about those limits, you can always place a stop order. If you leave standing instructions with your stockbroker, these are referred to as open orders that remain such until the transaction is executed and the order filled.

Try to set your limit orders just above the support levels (the lowest levels of value to which a stock can drop) and just below the level of resistance (the upper level above which it is difficult for the value of a stock to rise).

Also, set a value date – a date at which time you can take an average of the value of a particular commodity and review your options. This should be reviewed at least every six months, if you plan to retain any holdings of a particular security.

Chapter 13:

One Final Option

While "Chapter 13" is not an appropriate way to end a financial endeavor, it is, in this case, one of the most important conclusions to an incredibly helpful tool full of investment advice, especially when it is placed at the end of a book to offer assistance to those threatened with bankruptcy due to bad investment decisions.

There are always ways to turn around when you have begun to walk down the wrong path. Much like moving on to a new car after purchasing a lemon that has been nothing but a nightmare, you can reverse your direction.

Some people can spend days, months, and even years trying to conquer the stock market and still fail. In some cases, it is virtually impossible for an individual to ever get the hang of the functionality of the market. If you cannot follow market trends, then it is best that you do not make any investment decisions.

It is okay not to fit into the market. At the same time, you can still make money with investments. One final option you have is to create a discretionary account. This means that you sign a contract with your stockbroker and turn over a sum of money to the agent for investment, leaving the determination of placement of that investment in the hands of your agent. You never again have to worry that you have made a bad investment. In fact, in this scenario, you do not even have to follow any market trends or other information that has anything to do with financial investment. Your broker will simply let you know when you have increased your net worth or if your assets have taken a dive.

Whatever choices you make in regards to moving in on the stock market, you need not worry about not having the essential information to help you get through your first few trading experiences. Now, you have the basic knowledge and the essential reference guide to get you started on the path to success and wealth that you can access at any given time.

FREE COURSE: LEARN TO TRADE CURRENCY

http://fxtrade.oanda.com/learn/intro-to-currency-trading/

Currency Exchange, Forex, and FX – these are all terms used to describe the exchanging of one currency for another; for example, the exchanging of U.S. Dollars to British Pounds. In the foreign exchange market, this is viewed as buying pounds while simultaneously selling dollars.

Because two currencies are always involved, currencies are traded in the form of currency pairs, with the pricing based on the exchange rate offered by dealers in the forex market.

TABLE OF CONTENTS
- **Lesson 1: A Brief Introduction to the Currency Market**
- **Lesson 2: The Benefits of Trading Forex and Market Participants**
- **Lesson 3: Currency Trading Conventions - What You Need to Know before Trading**
- **Lesson 4: Making That First Trade**
- **Lesson 5: A Primer to Fundamental Analysis**
- **Lesson 6: An Introduction to Technical Analysis**
- **Prologue: A Final Word**

CPSIA information can be obtained
at www.ICGtesting.com
Printed in the USA
LVHW052031061021
699710LV00012B/1285